Jochen Knobloch

IM FLUG ÜBER IN FLIGHT OVER
FRANKFURT/MAIN und Umgebung

Mit einem Text von Sabine Beil

deutsch | englisch

Übersetzung: Martin Tümmler

HINSTORFF

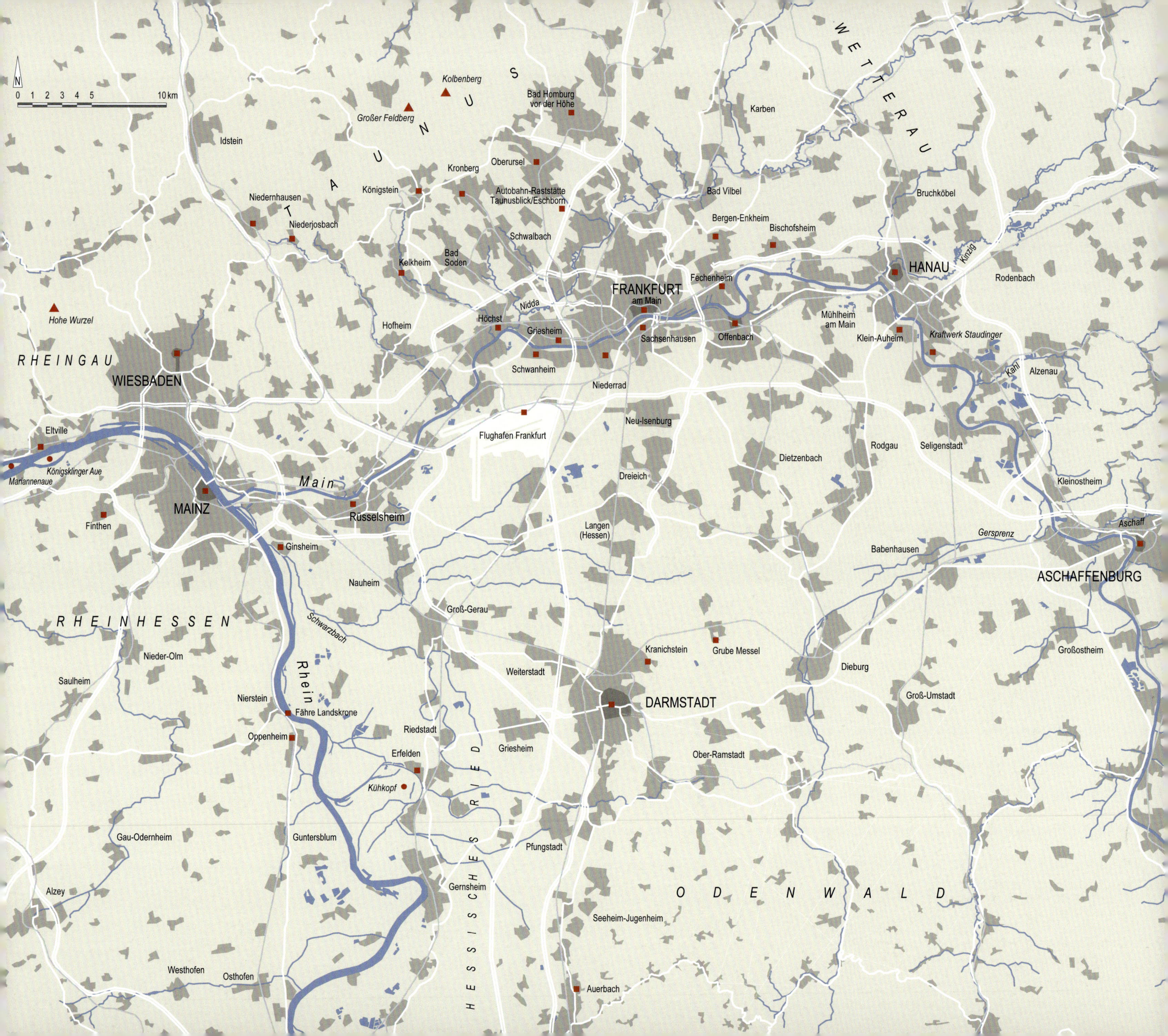
N
0 1 2 3 4 5 10 km
T A U N U S
W E T T E R A U
Kolbenberg
Großer Feldberg
Bad Homburg vor der Höhe
Idstein
Karben
Oberursel
Kronberg
Königstein
Autobahn-Raststätte Taunusblick/Eschborn
Bad Vilbel
Bruchköbel
Niedernhausen
Niederjosbach
Bergen-Enkheim
Bischofsheim
Schwalbach
Kelkheim
Bad Soden
Fechenheim
HANAU
Kinzig
Rodenbach
FRANKFURT am Main
Nidda
Höchst
Hohe Wurzel
Hofheim
Griesheim
Mühlheim am Main
Sachsenhausen
Offenbach
Klein-Auheim
Kraftwerk Staudinger
R H E I N G A U
WIESBADEN
Schwanheim
Kahl
Alzenau
Niederrad
Eltville
Neu-Isenburg
Flughafen Frankfurt
Rodgau
Seligenstadt
Königsklinger Aue
Mariannenaue
Dietzenbach
Main
Dreieich
MAINZ
Kleinostheim
Finthen
Rüsselsheim
Langen (Hessen)
Aschaff
Gersprenz
Ginsheim
Babenhausen
ASCHAFFENBURG
Nauheim
Groß-Gerau
R H E I N H E S S E N
Schwarzbach
Kranichstein
Grube Messel
Nieder-Olm
Großostheim
Rhein
Dieburg
Weiterstadt
Saulheim
Nierstein
DARMSTADT
Fähre Landskrone
Groß-Umstadt
Riedstadt
Oppenheim
Griesheim
Ober-Ramstadt
Erfelden
Kühkopf
Gau-Odernheim
Guntersblum
Pfungstadt
H E S S I S C H E S R I E D
Alzey
Gernsheim
O D E N W A L D
Seeheim-Jugenheim
Westhofen
Osthofen
Auerbach

Eine Kindheit im Taunus. Wälder, Felder, Wind. Viel Glatteis. Oft kommt der Schulbus nicht. Wenn doch, juckelt er ewig durchs kurvenreiche Wispertal. Schulbuskindheit: Wartezeit, Übelkeit. Motorradfahrer lieben diese Strecke. Ganze Gangs jagen dröhnend durch die grüne Beschaulichkeit. Fast jedes sonnige Wochenende lässt einer sein Leben. Auch die Autofahrer leben gefährlich. Wenn es auf der Bäderstraße kracht, dann richtig. Es wird nicht gefahren, sondern geheizt. Zeitungsfutter in der sonst ereignisarmen Gegend. Dann auch noch der rege Wildwechsel. Viele hatten schon mal ein Wildschwein vor dem Kühlergrill.

Sammeln. Pilze, Waldhimbeeren. Körbe-, eimerweise. Stille. Das Leben spielt anderswo. Auf dem vor sich hin rostenden Klettergerüst treffen sich die wenigen Heranwachsenden und schauen in die Luft. Der Himmel zerfurcht von Kondensstreifen. Wenigstens dort oben ein Hauch der großen weiten Welt. Irgendwo hinter vielen Höhenzügen liegt der Frankfurter Flughafen. Für Fluglärm zu weit weg. Zwei-, dreimal im Jahr Disco in der Dreschhalle. Eine Jugend im Untertaunus, zwischen Dickschied, Zorn und Watzelhain.

Das nächste Schwimmbad ist weit. Zum Einkaufen in die Stadt. Für alles braucht man ein Auto, die meisten haben aber nur eins, und das ist mit dem Vater auf der Arbeit. Also bleibt man Dorfinsasse, auf sich selbst gestellt. Keine aufwendigen Hobbies, kaum Ablenkung. Dorfdasein ohne Höhepunkte. Der größte Wunsch in dieser Zeit: Führerschein machen, ein eigenes Auto, raus hier!

Childhood in the Taunus. Forests, fields, wind. Lots of black ice. The school bus does not come all the time. When it does, it endlessly wobbles through the curvaceous Wispertal. School bus childhood: Waiting, nausea. Motorcyclists love this route. Whole gangs hound through the green tranquility with a rumble. Almost every sunny weekend someone perishes. Motorists are vulnerable as well. Every accident on this spa-road is serious. People are not driving, they are speeding. Sustenance for the newspaper in the otherwise uneventful area. Topping it off is the lively deer crossings. Many have already had a boar in front of the grille.

Gathering. Mushrooms, wild raspberries. By the basket and bucket full. Silence. Life takes place elsewhere. The few adolescents here meet by the rusty, decaying jungle gym and look up at the sky. The sky crisscrossed by contrails. At least up there is a whiff of the whole wide world. Somewhere, behind a range of hills, is the Frankfurt airport. Too far away for aircraft noise. Disco in the threshing-hall two or three times a year. Youth in the lower Taunus, between Dickschied, Zorn and Watzelhain.

The nearest swimming pool is far. In the city to go shopping. You need a car for everything, most will only have one, which is with the father at work. So, one stays village occupant, left to fend for oneself. No expensive hobbies, little distractions. Village life without highlights. The biggest wish at this time: get the driver's license, a car, get out of here!

Fährt man lange genug durch tiefe Wälder, bergauf, bergab, gelangt man nach Wiesbaden. Strahlende Bäderstadt mit heißen Quellen, mondänen Cafés, quirligem Markt und gediegener Kultur. Das einstige „Nizza des Nordens", Lieblingssommerfrische von Kaiser Wilhelm II., hatte Glück im Zweiten Weltkrieg und wurde nur zu einem Drittel zerstört. Für uns Landeier ist die Landeshauptstadt die erste urbane Herausforderung. Hier laufen lila Latzhosen herum und Friedensbewegte mit Palästinensertüchern. Aus den Boxen wummert die neue deutsche Welle, mit hennarotem Haar machen wir Abitur. Derweil geht in Frankfurt die Post ab. Ewiger Zankapfel: der Flughafen. Menschen wie du und ich errichten auf dem Gelände der umstrittenen Startbahn West ein Hüttendorf. Zehntausende demonstrieren gegen die Erweiterung, das Rhein-Main-Gebiet gerät in Wallung. Der Protest verbindet. Lässt die heterogene Region zusammenwachsen. Hält viele Menschen in Atem, bis heute. Die lärmgeplagten Anrainer des immer weiter wachsenden Frankfurt International Airport können ein leidvolles Lied davon singen.

Die nächste Uni für uns ist direkt auf der anderen Rheinseite in Mainz. Lernen auf einem Campus, der zuvor Kasernengelände war. Die katholische Domstadt fühlt sich bodenständig an, gemütlich, unverkrampft. Was sicher nicht nur an den vielen Studenten liegt, sondern auch an den ausgelassenen Festen, die hier gefeiert werden: Neben der meist lausig kalten Mainzer Fastnacht das oft mediterran anmutende Johannisfest im Sommer. Im Hintergrund Rheinhessen und Rheingau mit feinen Weinen. Radeln, Wandern, Paddeln – alles ist drin. Man muss es den alten Römern schon lassen: Sie hatten – zumindest für einige Zeit – ein unschlagbares Gespür für gute Gegenden. Über 300 Jahre waren sie hier und bauten den wohl berühmtesten Palissadenzaun der Weltgeschichte: den Limes, eine 550 Kilometer lange Grenzbefestigung, deren Überbleibsel seit 2005 UNESCO-Welterbe sind.

Siedlungsraum seit Jahrtausenden, heute extrem verdichtet mit Tendenz zum Verkehrsinfarkt. Überall Autobahnkreuze, Staus. Viel Zeit geht so verloren. Über unseren Köpfen starten und landen die Flieger im Minutentakt. Mittendrin die Heimat des „Doktorwagens". Hier, in einem Rüsselsheimer Kuhstall, baute Adam Opel erst Nähmaschinen, dann Fahrräder. Mit großherzoglicher Unterstützung von

If you drive long enough through thick forest, uphill, downhill, you arrive in Wiesbaden. Radiant spa-town with hot springs, swanky cafes, lively market and distinguished culture. The former "Nice of the north", favorite summer resort of Emperor Wilhelm II., was lucky during World War II as only one-third was destroyed. For us country bumpkins the state capital is the first urban challenge. This is where purple dungarees run around as well as peace activists with Palestinian scarves. Speakers blast the new German wave, we graduate with henna red hair. Meanwhile the action takes place in Frankfurt. Perpetual bone of contention: the airport. People like you and me are building a village of huts on the site of the controversial western runway. Tens of thousands demonstrate against the expansion, the Frankfurt Rhine-Main surges with emotion. The protest connects. The heterogeneous region grows closer together. Holds many people on tenterhooks even today. The noise-stricken residents of the ever-expanding Frankfurt international airport can sing this sorrowful song.

The next university for us is just on the other side of the Rhine in Mainz. Learning on a campus which was formerly a barracks. The catholic cathedral city feels traditional, cozy, relaxed. That is certainly not only due to the many students, but also the boisterous festivals that are celebrated: Not only the usually lousy cold Mainzer Fastnacht but also the often almost Mediterranean Johannisfest in the summer. In the background, Rheinhessen and Rheingau with fine wines. Biking, hiking, canoeing – anything is possible. You have to hand it to them: the Romans had – at least for some time – an unbeatable sense for good areas. They were here for a good 300 years, building the most famous palisade trench of world history: the Limes, a 550-kilometer border fortification. The remains are a UNESCO World Heritage site since 2005.

Am Schlossplatz in Wiesbaden liegt die Marktkirche. Sie überragt nicht nur das Rathaus der Landeshauptstadt, sondern auch den ihr gegenüber gelegenen Hessischen Landtag.

The Marktkirche (Market Church) is located by the Schlossplatz in Wiesbaden and does not only tower above the City Hall, but also the Hessian Parliament building on the opposite side.

Ernst Ludwig von Hessen und bei Rhein, seinerseits begeisterter Radler. Der Landesfürst, technikaffin und kunstsinnig, wird bald auch Automobilist. Als der erste PKW die Opel-Fabrik kurz vor der Jahrhundertwende verlässt, fährt er Tempo 20 und kommt auf stolze 3,5 PS.

Auf zur heimlichen Hauptstadt Deutschlands. „Wen Gott lieb hat, dem gibt er ein Haus in Frankfurt", sagt ein Sprichwort. Manche wären schon mit einer bezahlbaren Wohnung zufrieden, aber egal, Hauptsache Frankfurt. Die Leute lieben ihre Stadt, wollen nirgends anders sein, warum auch, hier haben sie ja alles. Zeitgeschehen zum Anfassen. Menschen, die sich nicht unterkriegen lassen. Viel kritische Masse, schon immer, bis hin zur Occupy-Bewegung. Hochkarätige Kultur, ein Fluss mit viel Freizeitpotenzial, Natur satt in Reichweite. Eine futuristische Skyline, ein bisschen Altstadtfeeling, Boomtown mit Kuschelfaktor. Überbordende Messen mit Menschen aus aller Welt. Und mittendrin Äppelwoi, serviert im Bembelsche, in gemütlichen Fachwerkschänken in Sachsenhausen. Dazu Handkäs´ mit Musik oder Pellkartoffeln mit grüner Soße, angeblich Goethes Lieblingsessen.

Frankfurt, Bankfurt, Mainhattan. Stadt der Superlative, Metropole im Herzen Europas, schon immer. Hier steht die Paulskirche, „Wiege der Demokratie" und eines der ersten Gebäude Deutschlands, das in den Genuss einer Zentralheizung kam. Fast wäre Frankfurt 1949 tatsächlich Hauptstadt geworden, hat dann aber gegen Bonn der Kürzeren gezogen. Das bereits vorgesehene Parlamentsgebäude beheimatet bis heute den Hessischen Rundfunk. Politik wird trotzdem gemacht. Längst hat sich Frankfurt zum wichtigsten Finanzplatz Kontinentaleuropas gemausert. Hier sitzen weltweit agierende Geldverwalter, hier brodelt die Börse.

Abgründe. Tiefschürfend der heftige Streit rund um eine stillgelegte Ölschiefergrube im kleinen Weiler Messel bei Darmstadt. Die Grube sollte Mülldeponie werden, doch dann fanden Forscher ungewöhnlich gut erhaltene Fossilien aus dem Eozän. Der zermürbende Kampf um dieses einzigartige Fenster zur Erdgeschichte dauerte 20 Jahre, kostete mehr als 65 Millionen Mark und ging durch alle Instanzen. Seit 1995 ist das wohl berühmteste Müllkippenprojekt der Republik UNESCO-Weltnaturerbe und ein Besuchermagnet der Region. Mit Urpferdchen Ida als Maskottchen: Tiere wie dieses wurden so groß wie ein Hund.

Settlement area for thousands of years, today extremely compact verging on gridlock. Interchanges everywhere, traffic jams. Lots of time burned. Planes take off and land every minute over our heads. In the middle of it all the home of the "doctor's car". Here, in a cowshed in Rüsselsheim, Adam Opel first built sewing machines, then bicycles. With generous grand-ducal support from Ernst Ludwig of Hesse and by Rhine, an avid cyclist. The prince, with a nose for technology and art, will soon also be a motorist. The first car leaves the Opel factory shortly before the turn of the century, with a top speed of 20 km / h and an impressive 3.5 hp.

Onto the secret capital of Germany. "Whom God loves, he gives a house in Frankfurt" as the saying goes. Some would be content with an affordable apartment, but that is insignificant as long as it's in Frankfurt. People love their city, do not want to be anywhere else, and why would they, they have everything here. Current affairs to touch. People who won't let themselves be put down. Lots of critical mass, always, including the occupy movement. Top-class culture, a river with a lot of recreational potential, abundant nature within reach. A futuristic skyline, a little old town feel, boomtown with native charm. Overflowing fairs with people from all over the world. And in the middle: cider, served in a Bembel (special pitcher) in a cozy timbered tavern in Sachsenhausen. Also served with Handkäs´ (sour milk cheese) with music or boiled potatoes with green sauce, supposedly Goethe's favorite food.

Frankfurt, Bankfurt, Mainhattan. City of superlatives, metropolis at the heart of Europe, since forever. Home to St. Paul's Church, "cradle of democracy" and one of the first buildings in Germany, which benefited from central heating. Frankfurt actually almost became the capital in 1949, but drew the short straw against Bonn. The provided parliament building is home to the Hessian Radio to this day. Nevertheless politics. Frankfurt has blossomed into the major financial center in continental Europe long ago. This is where global money managers sit, where the commotion of the stock exchange is.

Abyss. The profoundly fierce dispute of a shutdown oil shale pit in the small hamlet Messel near Darmstadt. The pit was going to be a waste diposal site, but then researchers found unusually well preserved fossils from the Eocene. The grueling battle for this unique

Nur ein paar Steinwürfe entfernt liegt Hanau, meine Geburtsstadt und die der Brüder Grimm. Die beiden waren unermüdliche Sammler, im ganzen Hessenland trugen sie Märchen zusammen und schrieben sie auf. Damit nicht genug, auch das bis dahin größte und umfassendste Wörterbuch der deutschen Sprache verdanken wir ihnen – das erste Kompendium übrigens, in dem auch Schimpfwörter Platz fanden.

Der wohl berühmteste Hesse spazierte von seinem Frankfurter Elternhaus aus gerne durch die Lande. Legendär seine Ausflüge ins benachbarte Darmstadt, wo er den Schriftsteller Johann Heinrich Merck und einen Kreis von „Empfindsamen" traf. Was Goethe unterwegs auf den 25 Kilometern erlebte, inspirierte ihn zu Gedichten wie „Wanderers Sturmlied". Darmstadt war auch der Grund, warum er seinen späteren Arbeitgeber und Freund kennenlernte: Herzog Carl August von Sachsen-Weimar. Dieser wollte um die Hand von Prinzessin Luise von Hessen-Darmstadt anhalten. Als er seine künftigen Schwiegereltern besuchte, nutzte er die Reise gleich dazu, den sturm- und drangvollen Autor des „Werther" kennenzulernen.

Überhaupt, die Darmstädter Prinzessinnen! Auf dem internationalen Heiratsmarkt spielten sie eine herausragende Rolle. Die Töchter aus dem Hause Hessen-Darmstadt eigneten sich bestens für adelige Allianzen. Auch die letzte Zarin stammt aus Darmstadt. 1894 heiratete Prinzessin Alix den russischen Kronprinzen Nikolaus. Als Zarin Alexandra Fjodorowna ging sie in die Geschichte ein. 1918 wurde sie mit ihrer ganzen Familie in den Wirren der russischen Revolution erschossen.

Im nahen Fürstenlager Auerbach hatten sich die beiden einst kennengelernt. Ein denkbar exotischer Landschaftspark samt eigenem Dorf, den sich die Landgrafen von Hessen-Darmstadt 1790 erbauen ließen. Zwecks Erquickung, und um dem einfachen Landleben fern höfischer Etikette zu frönen, wie es damals Mode war. Egal, ob die Lustwandelnden unter sich blieben oder Staatsbesuch zugegen war: Das einfache Volk konnte sie beim Picknicken beobachten, sah sie auf den Wiesen lagern – daher der Name „Fürstenlager". Bis heute ist dieser besondere Ort eines der beliebtesten Ausflugsziele an der hessischen Bergstraße.

Da die Romanows ihre Sommer gern in Südhessen verbrachten, ließ der frisch vermählte Zar Nikolaus II. für sich und seinen Hofstaat

window into Earth's history took 20 years, cost more than 65 million marks and went through all the courts. The probably most famous landfill project of the republic is a UNESCO world heritage site since 1995 and a major attraction for the region. Along with the ancient horse Ida as mascot: animals such as this grew to the size of dogs.

Hanau is only a few stone throws away, my birthplace and that of the brothers Grimm. Both were tireless collectors, gathering fairy tales from throughout Hesse and writing them down. Not only that, even the then largest and most comprehensive dictionary of the German language, is owed to them – the first compendium by the way, which contained swearwords.

The probably most famous Hesse enjoyed walks from his Frankfurter childhood home to the surrounding countryside. His visits to the nearby Darmstadt are legendary, where he met the writer Johann Heinrich Merck and a group of "sentimentalists". Goethe was inspired by his travels on the 25 kilometer route, writing poems such as "Wanderer's Storm Song". Darmstadt was also the reason why he met his later employer and friend: Duke Carl August of Saxony-Weimar, who wanted to propose to the Princess Luise of Hesse-Darmstadt. While visiting his future in-laws, he used the journey to get to know the storm and stress author of "Werther".

These Darmstadt princesses! They played a prominent role on the international wedding market. The daughters of the house of Hesse-Darmstadt were perfectly suited for aristocratic alliances. The last tsarina also comes from Darmstadt. Princess Alix married the Russian crown prince in 1894. She went down in history as Tsarina Alexandra Feodorovna. She was shot, along with her entire family in the turmoil of the Russian Revolution in 1918.

The two first met in the nearby Fürstenlager of Auerbach. A picturesque an exotically landscaped park including a private village, which the landgraves of Hesse-Darmstadt built in 1790. As an area of refreshment, and to indulge in simple country life away from courtly etiquette, as fashionable at the time. Whether they were strolling and keeping to themselves or state visitors were present: The common people could observe them picnicking, see them lay down in the meadows (the name Fürstenlager is a German play on words, as they were encamping (Lagern) the meadows). This particular loca-

eine russische Kapelle auf der Mathildenhöhe in Darmstadt bauen, errichtet auf eigens herbeigeschaffter russischer Erde. Direkt daneben gründete sein kunstsinniger Schwager, wiederum Großherzog Ernst Ludwig, Bruder der letzten Zarin, 1899 die Darmstädter Künstlerkolonie und machte die Stadt zum Zentrum des Jugendstils. Sein Leitspruch, „Mein Hessenland blühe und in ihm die Kunst", trägt Früchte bis heute. Der Musenhügel mit Hochzeitsturm und Platanenhain wurde jüngst in die deutsche Vorschlagsliste für das UNESCO-Welterbe aufgenommen.

Darmstadt, die große Unbekannte. Die oft Übersehene, Belächelte. Die sich einst stolz „Stadt im Walde" nannte, was man aus der Vogelperspektive noch heute nachvollziehen kann. Jeweils am 11. September, meinem Geburtstag, läuten hier um Mitternacht alle Kirchenglocken. Ein Himmelskonzert, das durch Mark und Bein geht. Erinnert es doch an den Bombenangriff der Alliierten im Jahr 1944. Die britischen Piloten sollten seinerzeit Dresden anfliegen. Doch dann wurde es Darmstadt und die einst prächtige Residenz wurde in Schutt und Asche gelegt. Heute steht Darmstadt für Kunst und Wissenschaft. Hier wirken die Fraunhofer Gesellschaft, die Technische Universität, das Europäische Raumflugkontrollzentrum – und neuerdings ereignen sich sogar Fußballwunder.

„Geht einmal nach Darmstadt", forderte Georg Büchner, der Revolutionär mit Feder und Skalpell, dessen aufreibendes Leben schon mit 23 Jahren zu Ende war. Einst floh er des Nachts aus seinem Elternhaus in der Darmstädter Altstadt vor seinen Häschern, heute steht dort ein Bioladen. Prophetisch seine politischen Thesen, gültig und aktuell bis heute. „Friede den Hütten! Krieg den Palästen", so der Slogan des Hessischen Landboten – unlängst wieder von den "Occupy"-Aktivisten zitiert.

Frankfurt war immer schon ein Machtzentrum, kapitalträchtig. Heute hat es einen üppigen Speckgürtel, der vom Taunus bis nach Bensheim reicht. Macht und Reichtum – die Kehrseiten liegen auf der Hand. Wo viel Licht, da auch viel Schatten.

Meist wonnig ist das Wetter in der Region. Der Rheingau und die Bergstraße zählen zu den mildesten Gegenden Deutschlands. Im Frühjahr Spargel- und Erdbeerfelder, wohin man schaut. In der Ferne der Odenwald, Heimat der Nibelungensage. In der Rheinebene das

tion is one of the most popular getaway destinations along the Hessian mountain road to date.

Since the Romanovs enjoyed spending their summers in southern Hesse, the newly-married Czar Nicholas II. had a Russian chapel built in Mathildenhöhe by Darmstadt, even acquiring Russian soil just for the construction. His art-loving brother-in-law, Grand Duke Ernst Ludwig, brother of the last tsarina, established the Darmstadt artists' colony in 1899 right next to the chapel, making the city the center of Art Nouveau. His motto, "Let my Hesse flourish just as the art within Hesse", is bearing fruit even today. The muse-hill with its wedding tower (Hochzeitsturm) and plane tree grove (Platanenhain) was recently taken into the German suggestion list for UNESCO World Heritage sites.

Darmstadt, the great unknown. The often overlooked, belittled. The once proudly self-proclaimed "city in the forest", which is understandable with a bird's eye view. On the 11th of September, my birthday, the church bells ring every year at midnight. A concert in the sky, which touches you to the core. A reminder of the Allied bombing raid in 1944. The British pilots were meant to fly to Dresden. But then it changed to Darmstadt and the once magnificent residence was reduced to rubble. Today Darmstadt embodies art and science. This is where the Fraunhofer Institute, the Technical University, the European Space Operations Centre operate – and recently even football miracles occur.

"Go to Darmstadt once in a while", demands Georg Büchner, the revolutionary with pen and scalpel whose exhausting life was already at its end after 23 years. He once fled from his childhood-home in the historic center of Darmstadt from his pursuers at night, now there is an organic grocery store there. His political theses are prophetic, valid and relevant today. "Peace to the shacks! War on the palaces", the slogan of the Hessian courier - recently cited by the "occupy"-activists.

Mittelpunkt der Innenstadt von Darmstadt ist der Luisenplatz (im Vordergrund).

The central point of downtown Darmstadt is the Luisenplatz (in the foreground).

Hessische Ried mit seinem Naturschutzgebiet Kühkopf: ein kleines Paradies, für Menschen wie Mücken. Rund um die duftende Knoblochsaue haben Schnaken ideale Brutstätten für sich entdeckt. Nun rückt alljährlich eine kommunale Aktionsgemeinschaft zur Bekämpfung der Plage aus.

Unbilden der Natur, schweres Erbe der Geschichte: Immer wieder ist auch der Kampfmittelräumdienst gefordert. Überall lauern noch Bomben aus dem Zweiten Weltkrieg im Boden: besonders auf Industrieanlagen, Bahnhöfen oder dem Flughafengelände. Für ihre lebensgefährliche Arbeit nutzen die Entschärfer Luftaufnahmen der Alliierten: Sobald sich die Rauchschwaden nach dem Abwurf der Bomben verzogen hatten, kamen die Aufklärungsflugzeuge, um das Ergebnis festzuhalten. Diese alten Bilder sind von hervorragender Qualität. Besonders besorgniserregend eine historische Alliiertenaufnahme des Frankfurter Flughafens: ein einziger Bombenteppich wird dort sichtbar. Bis heute lassen die Verantwortlichen jeden Zentimeter überprüfen, bei geplanten Erweiterungen werden die Daten aktualisiert, frei gegebene Flächen grün schraffiert. So kann er denn weiterwachsen, der Airport.

Fliegen. Bilder aus der Vogelperspektive? Ausgerechnet in Kronberg im Taunus sind die ersten privaten Luftbildaufnahmen der Welt entstanden. Ersonnen 1904 vom findigen Apotheker Julius Neubronner, der ursprünglich nur seine Rezepte, später auch leichte Medikamente via Brieftaube verschickt – Vorläufer heutiger Transportdrohnen. Später versieht der Apotheker seine Luftboten mit kleinen, selbstgebauten Kameras inklusive automatischem Auslösemechanismus. Seine Idee der Brieftaubenfotografie wird prämiert. Wen wundert´s, dass sich bald auch das Militär dafür interessiert ...

Die Region schreibt deutsche Luftfahrtgeschichte. Schon 1802 bestaunt der Hessische Hof zu Darmstadt einen bemannten „Luft-Ballon", der bis auf 20 Schuh hochsteigt. Ein Jahrhundert später tummeln sich hier die tollkühnen Männer mit ihren fliegenden Kisten: Der älteste Flugplatz Deutschlands liegt nicht etwa in Frankfurt, sondern in Darmstadt, am Griesheimer Sand, gegründet 1908 von August Euler. Der war Luftfahrtpionier in mehrfacher Hinsicht: Er richtete die erste deutsche Flugschule und die erste Fabrik für Motorflugzeuge ein. Als Erster erwirbt er ein internationales Pilotenpatent und erhält

Frankfurt has always been a center of power, infused with capital. Today it has a lush, affluent suburbs ranging from Taunus up to Bensheim. Power and wealth – the downsides are obvious. Where a lot of light, there is also plenty of shade.

The weather in the region is most delightful. The Rheingau and the Bergstraße are among the mildest parts of Germany. Asparagus and strawberry fields in spring, wherever you look. In the distance, the Odenwald, home of the Nibelungen saga. In the Rhine valley, the Hessian Ried with its nature reserve Kühkopf: a little paradise for people and mosquitoes. Around the fragrant Knoblochsaue gnats have discovered an ideal breeding ground for themselves. To combat the scourge, a local action group moves out every year.

Ravages of nature, difficult legacy of history: time and again the bomb disposal unit is required. Bombs from the Second World War are still lurking in the ground everywhere: especially by industrial plants, railway stations, or the airport. The bomb disposal officers rely on aerial images from the Allies for their dangerous work: once the smoke had cleared after the bombs were dropped the reconnaissance aircraft flew overhead to capture the results. These old photos are of excellent quality. Especially alarming are the historic recordings of the Allies for the Frankfurt airport: it shows a single carpet of bombs. Even today the authorities have to have every centimeter checked, the data is updated for planned extensions, cleared areas shaded green. All so he can continue to grow, our airport.

Flight. Pictures from a bird's eye view? The first private aerial images of the world where created in Kronberg in the Taunus of all places. Devised in 1904 by a resourceful pharmacist named Julius Neubronner, who originally only sent his recipes, later small amounts of medication via carrier pigeon – forerunner of today's transport drones. Later, the pharmacist provided his aerial messengers with small, self-built cameras including an automatic trigger mechanism. His idea of pigeon photography was awarded a prize. It's no surprise that the military also developed an interest soon after ...

The region goes down in German aviation history. As early as 1802 is when the Hessian court Darmstadt marveled at a manned "air balloon", which rose to a height of 20 shoes. A century later and the area is bustling with daring men and their flying machines: The oldest airfield

das Flugzeugführer-Zeugnis „Deutschland Nr. 1". Sein berühmtester Schüler ist Prinz Heinrich von Preußen, der Bruder des Deutschen Kaisers. Auch hier ist der Darmstädter Großherzog Ernst Ludwig großzügiger Unterstützer, und mit ihm seine Gemahlin Eleonore, die selbst gern im Eulerschen Zweisitzer mitfliegt. Als der Griesheimer Sand aus allen Nähten platzt, zieht Euler 1912 nach Frankfurt-Niederrad um. Und erst damit beginnt die Geschichte des Frankfurter Flughafens. Ausgerechnet bei einem Flugzeugabsturz kommt Eleonore 1937 ums Leben und mit ihr fast die gesamte großherzogliche Familie.

Frankfurt/Rhein-Main: Die Gegend könnte snobby sein, ist sie aber nicht. Kann sie auch nicht wirklich, das Hessische lässt grüßen. Das weiche „t" macht alles „inderessand", und sanft schmilzt das „p" im „Dibbsche" dahin. Egal, wohin es einen verschlägt: Diese Wurzeln lassen sich nicht verleugnen. Und das ist auch gut so, weil lustig. Mainz, Wiesbaden, Frankfurt: eine Gegend, die Heinz Schenk und die Rodgau Monotones hervorgebracht hat – und natürlich Badesalz. Auf jeden Fall eine Gegend, in die man immer wieder gern zurückkehrt.

„Franckfurt bleibt das Nest", lästerte der junge Goethe und verließ das „leidig Loch" mit 26 Jahren, um künftig sein Wesen im viel kleineren Weimar zu treiben. Im Alter gab er sich milder: „Wenn mich jemand früge, wo ich mir den Platz meiner Wiege bequemer, meiner bürgerlichen Gesinnung gemäßer oder poetischen Ansicht entsprechender denke, ich könnte keine liebere Stadt als Frankfurt nennen."

Mich selbst hat es inzwischen nach Niedersachsen verschlagen. Wie es mir hier geht? Niemand hätte es treffender formulieren können als wiederum Goethe, der seinen Mephistopheles im Faust II sagen lässt:

„Man denkt an das, was man verließ;
Was man gewohnt war, bleibt ein Paradies."

Sabine Beil

in Germany is not in Frankfurt, but in Darmstadt, by the Griesheimer Sand, founded in 1908 by August Euler. An aviation pioneer in several ways: He established the first German aviation school and the first factory for motorized airplanes. He was the first to acquire an international pilot license and received the license "Germany No.1". His most famous pupil is Prince Henry of Prussia, brother of the German Emperor. Again, the Darmstadt Grand Duke Ernst Ludwig is a generous supporter, and with him his wife Eleonore, who enjoyed flying in the Euler two-seater. As the Griesheimer Sand was bursting at the seams, Euler moved to Frankfurt-Niederrad in 1912. That is only the beginning of the history of the Frankfurt airport. In a plane crash Eleonore perishes in 1937, along with most of the grand ducal family.

Frankfurt/Rhine-Main: The area could be snobby, but it is not. Can't really be, the Hessian aspect comes through. The soft "t" makes everything "inderesding", and the "p" in "Dibbsche" gently melts away. Wherever one ends up: These roots cannot be denied. And that's a good thing, because funny. Mainz, Wiesbaden, Frankfurt: an area that produced Heinz Schenk (television entertainer) and the Rodgau Monotones (Rockband singing hessian slang) – and of course Badesalz (a famous german comedy duo). Definitely an area one always enjoys returning to.

"Franckfurt remains the nest" railed the young Goethe, left the "annoying hole" with 26 years and continued going about his spirited life in the much smaller Weimar. In his old age he reminisced milder: "If someone asked me where I would be more comfortable placing my cradle, according to my civic mindedness or poetic views, I could not name any dearer city than Frankfurt."

Myself, I have wound up in Lower Saxony. How I'm doing here? Once again no one could have put it more aptly than Goethe, who has his Mephistopheles in Faust II say:

"One thinks of all one's left: besides,
What one's used to is paradise."

Sabine Beil

Anflug von Südwesten: Der Blick geht über Raunheim und den Flughafen Richtung Frankfurter Innenstadt.
Approaching from the southwest: The view reaches from Raunheim to the airport and onwards toward downtown Frankfurt.

Unmittelbar am Flughafen Frankfurt erstreckt sich The Squaire, ein futuristisch gestalteter Bürokomplex.
The Squaire, a futuristic office complex, spreads out directly by the Frankfurt Aiport.

Markant ragen die Türme des Frankfurter Bankenviertels in den Himmel.
The towers of Frankfurt's financial district protrude sharply into the sky.

Seit Ende des 19. Jahrhunderts ist er einer der wichtigsten Eisenbahnknotenpunkte Europas: der Hauptbahnhof in Frankfurt.

Since the late 19th century, it has been one of the most important railway hubs in Europe: the Main Station in Frankfurt

Bahnhof und Bahnhofsvorplatz: Auf dem Dach des Empfangsgebäudes trägt seit über 125 Jahren ein bronzener Atlas die Erdkugel.

Train station and forecourt: On the roof of the station building a bronze Atlas has been carrying the globe for more than 125 years.

Der Westhafen Tower überragt seit 2004 das direkt am Main gelegene Gutleutviertel.
The Westhafentower has been dominating the Gutleut-district since 2004.

Zwischen Hauptbahnhof und Main liegt der Baseler Platz, dominiert durch das sogenannte Oval, das auch 2004 vollendet wurde.
The Baseler Platz, between the Central Station and Main, is being dominated by the so-called Oval, which was also completed in 2004.

UBS
UBS

Im Gegensatz zu Paris oder London liegt das Hochhausviertel von Frankfurt in unmittelbarer Nachbarschaft zur historischen Innenstadt.

In contrast to Paris or London, the high-rise district of Frankfurt is an immediate neighbor by the historic inner city.

Von der Paulskirche (rechts) bis zu den ersten Bankentürmen sind es nur wenige Gehminuten.
From St. Paul's Church (right) – the first bank towers are within walking distance.

Neben der Hauptwache, die einem der zentralen Plätze Frankfurts den Namen gab, liegt die Katharinenkirche.
Next to the Hauptwache, after which one of the central squares of Frankfurt is named, is St. Catherine's Church.

Zwischen der Großen Eschenheimer Straße und der Zeil befindet sich seit 2010 das Palaisquartier ...
Between the Große Eschenheimer Straße and the Zeil is where, since 2010, the Palais Quartier is located ...

… Es umfasst mehrere Hochhäuser und das Einkaufszentrums My Zeil.

… It includes several high-rise buildings and the shopping mall My Zeil.

Die bewegt wirkende Fassaden- und Dachgestaltung von My Zeil setzt ein auffälliges Zeichen an Frankfurts bekanntester Einkaufsmeile.

The facade and roof design of My Zeil almost seems to be moving, setting a distinctive mark on Frankfurt's most famous shopping street.

Trotz starker Kriegszerstörung weist das Zentrum Frankfurts wichtige historische Gebäude auf: die Bartholomäus-Kirche, auch Frankfurter Dom genannt (links), den Römer (Bildmitte) und die Paulskirche (rechts).

Despite extensive destruction during the war, the heart of Frankfurt still contains many important historical buildings: the Bartholomew Church, also known as the Frankfurt Cathedral (left), the Roman (center), St. Paul's Church (right).

Die Paulskirche gilt als die Wiege der deutschen Demokratie. Hier tagte 1848/49 das erste frei gewählte Parlament hierzulande.
St. Paul's Church, the cradle of German democracy. The first freely elected parliament in these parts was in session here in 1848/49.

Frankfurt besteht nicht nur aus Stein, Asphalt, Glas und Beton, sondern weist auch viele Grünflächen auf – so im Gebiet um die Bleichstraße.

Frankfurt is not just stone, asphalt, concrete and glass, there are also many green spaces – like the area around the Bleichstraße.

Einer der bekanntesten Grünzüge der Stadt ist die Taunusanlage, die vom Taunustor bis zur Alten Oper (rechts oben) reicht.

One of the most known green areas of the city is the Taunusanlage, ranging from the Taunusgate to the Old Opera (top right).

Um die Jahrtausendwende entstand nahe der Alten Oper „Die Welle". Der Geschäfts- und Wohnkomplex ist zwar nicht so hoch wie der dahinter liegende Opernturm, aber trotzdem architektonisch markant.

Around the turn of the millennium was when "Die Welle" (The Wave) took on form near the Old Opera. While the commercial and residential complex is not as high as the Opera Tower behind it, it's architecturally striking nevertheless.

Das Westend gewinnt alljährlich mehr an Höhe.
The Westend gains in height every year.

Eines der neusten Hochhäuser Frankfurts ist der Taunusturm – nahe dem Commerzbank Tower gelegen (rechts), der mit 259 Metern das höchste Bürogebäude der Stadt darstellt.

One of the newest skyscrapers of Frankfurt is the Taunusturm (Taunus Tower) – located near the Commerzbank Tower (right), which is the tallest office building in the city with 259 meters.

Seit kurzer Zeit überragt der Sitz der Europäischen Zentralbank das Ostend und das Gebiet um den Osthafen.
Recently, the seat of the European Central Bank surpasses the Ostend district and the area around the eastern harbor.

Der Blick über die Innenstadt von Frankfurt reicht vom Messeturm bis zu dem im Bildhintergrund am Main gelegenen EZB-Tower.
The view over downtown Frankfurt reaches from the Messeturm (Exhibition Tower) all the way to the ECB Tower in the background.

Am östlichen Rand von Sachsenhausen liegt seit 2008 der Main Triangel – ein bemerkenswert modernes Ambiente für die hier beheimatete Oberfinanzdirektion.

The Main Triangle is located on the eastern edge of Sachsenhausen since 2008 – a remarkably modern feel for the home of the Oberfinanzdirektion (a governmental institution for finance).

Zwei Hochhaustürme und eine ehemalige Großmarkthalle sind seit 2015 Sitz der Europäischen Zentralbank.

Two high-rise towers and a former wholesale store are the seat of the European Central Bank since 2015.

COMING SOON
WINX

Zwischen der Innenstadt und Sachsenhausen mit dem Museumsufer fließt der Main, ohne den es die erste Besiedlung und die spätere Stadtwerdung nicht gegeben hätte.

Between the downtown area and Sachsenhausen with the "Museumsufer" where the river Main flows, without which the first settlements and the later growth into a city would not have been possible.

Hinter dem Gebiet um den Oeder Weg türmt sich der Gebäudekomplex des Palais Quartiers auf. Rechts daneben verschwinden fast die früheren Dominaten Katharinenkirche und Eschenheimer Turm

Behind the area around the Oeder way the building complex of the Palais Quartier towers higher and higher, St. Catherine's Church and the Eschenheimer Tower (on the right), which dominated earlier, almost disappear.

Aus dem 15. Jahrhundert stammt
die Bockenheimer Warte,
ein Wehrturm.

The Bockenheimer Warte, a fortified tower, dates back to the 15th century.

Seit 1871 gibt es den
im Stadtteil Westend
liegenden Palmengarten.

The Palm Garden has been in the Westend district since 1871.

Die Ursprünge des Frankfurter Zoos gehen auf das Jahr 1858 zurück, als Bürger der Stadt begannen, ihn auf Probe zu betreiben. Bald war klar, dass der Tierpark zu einer festen Einrichtung werden sollte.

The origins of the Frankfurt Zoo date back to the year 1858, when citizens of the city began operating it on a trial basis. It soon became clear that the Zoological Garden should be a permanent establishment.

„Tiere erleben – Natur bewahren", so lautet des Motto des Zoos, der mitten in der Stadt – im Ostend – liegt.
"Experience Animals – Preserve Nature" is the motto of the zoo, which is in the middle of the city – in the Ostend district.

Der repräsentative Eingang zum Zoo befindet sich am Alfred-Brehm-Platz.
The representative entrance to the Zoo is located by the Alfred Brehm-Platz.

Im Nordend steht seit gut 100 Jahren die neoromanisch gestaltete Kirche St. Bernhard.
The Neo-Romanesque church St. Bernard can be found in the Nordend district for about 100 years.

Direkt am Messegelände und nahe dem knapp 257 Meter hohen Messeturm mit seinem Pyramidendach entstand in den letzten Jahren das Skyline Plaza, ein großes Einkaufszentrum.

Right beside the exhibition grounds and the almost 257 meter high Messeturm with its pyramid roof, the Skyline Plaza emerged in recent years.

Das Messegelände in Frankfurt, das auch die kuppelförmige Festhalle einschließt, ist alljährlich Schauplatz der größten Buchmesse der Welt.

The exhibition grounds in Frankfurt, which also include the dome-shaped Festhalle are the annual venue of the biggest book fair in the world.

Vielfältig ist die Dachgestaltung des Skyline Plaza.

The rooftop design of the Skyline Plaza is multifaceted.

Zwischen Bockenheimer Warte und Messegelände erstreckt sich die Senckenberganlage.

Senckenberganlage extends between Bockenheimer Warte and the exhibition grounds.

Seit 1997 stehen sie direkt am Messegelände: die Hochhäuser „Kastor" (vorne) und „Pollux".

Located right at the front of the exhibition grounds since 1997: the skyscrapers „Kastor" (in the front) and „Pollux".

Gleichfalls Teil des Messegeländes ist der Rundbau des Congress Centers an der Ludwig-Erhard-Anlage.
The rotunda of the Congress Center at the Ludwig-Erhard-Anlage is also part of the exhibition grounds.

1984 entstand das Messe Torhaus, in dessen rötliche Steinfassade ein die Umgebung spiegelnder Glas-Corpus eingeschoben ist.
The exhibition gatehouse, with a reddish stone facade and a glass corpus, which mirrors the surrounding, was built in 1984.

Wohnbebauung, Verkehrswege, Bürokomplexe – in vielen Stadtteilen Frankfurts mischen sich, wie hier beim Messegelände, Bauwerke mit unterschiedlichen Funktionen.

Residential buildings, traffic routes, office buildings – in many parts of Frankfurt's districts different functional buildings mix, just like here at the exhibition grounds.

ibc

Aus allen Himmelsrichtungen ist es beeindruckend: das Panorama der Frankfurter Innenstadt, hier von Westen gesehen, mit dem Messegelände im Vordergrund.

Impressive from all directions: the panorama of downtown Frankfurt, as seen here from the west, with the exhibition grounds in the foreground.

Von oben erinnert es etwas an die Olympiabauten in München: das Rebstockbad, größtes Hallenbad Frankfurts.

From above it is somewhat reminiscent of the Olympic buildings in Munich: the Rebstockbad, the largest indoor pool of Frankfurt.

Ist es beim Rebstockbad die zeltartige Dachkonstruktion, die das Gebäude prägt, so fällt das nahe gelegene Radisson Blu durch seine runde Scheibenform ins Auge.

The Rebstockbad building is characterized by its tent-like roof structure, while the nearby Radisson Blu has an eye-catching disk shape.

An das Rebstockbad schließt sich ein Volkspark an. Dass sich hier einst der erste Frankfurter Flughafen befand, ist heute nicht mehr erkennbar.

A public park adjoins the Rebstockbad. Frankfurt's first airport was once located here, now just a memory.

Die wirtschaftliche Bedeutung der Schifffahrt für Frankfurt, aber auch für das südlich des Main gelegene Offenbach, zeigt sich unter anderem in der Größe der Häfen – hier ein Teil des Osthafens.

The economic importance of shipping for Frankfurt as well as Offenbach, located in thr south of the Main, becomes evident in the size of the ports – here an image of the eastern harbor.

Am Südbecken des Osthafens hat die moderne Zeit in Form eines Container-Terminals Einzug gehalten.

At the southern basin of the eastern harbor, modern times have arrived in the form of a container terminal.

Dass nicht nur Hochhäuser wie die EZB-Zentrale das Bild der Region dominieren, sondern auch der Main landschaftsprägend ist, zeigt sich gerade in den Spiegelungen bei Gegenlicht.

The image of the region is not only dominated by the skyscrapers, such as the ECB headquarters – the Main also shapes the landscape, which becomes particularly evident in the reflections in the contre-jour style picture.

Über den Main und Fechenheim geht der Blick Richtung Westen zur Frankfurter Innenstadt.

Across the Main and Fechenheim the view turns westward to downtown Frankfurt.

Offenbach mit seinen gut 120 000 Einwohnern kann auf eine über tausendjährige Geschichte zurückblicken.

Offenbach with its 120,000 inhabitants can look back on over a thousand years of history.

Die A 66, hier bei Bergen-Enkheim, ist einer von zahlreichen Verkehrswegen, die in und durch das Rhein-Main-Gebiet führen.

The A 66, here at Bergen-Enkheim, is one of many roads leading into and through the Rhine-Main area.

Auch Bischofsheim liegt an der A 66.

Bischofsheim is also located on the A66.

Während Bürgel (im Bildvordergrund) zu Offenbach gehört, ist das am anderen Mainufer gelegene Fechenheim seit 1928 ein Stadtteil von Frankfurt.

While Bürgel (in the foreground) is a part of Offenbach, Fechenheim, located on the other bank of the Main, has been a district of Frankfurt since 1928.

Die Innenstadt von Offenbach liegt an einem der schönsten Flussbögen, die der Main auf seinem Weg in den Rhein gebildet hat.

Downtown Offenbach is located on one of the most beautiful river arcs, eroded by the Main on its way to the Rhine.

Märchenhaft wirken Schloss und Park Philippsruhe in Hanau, jener Stadt, in der die Brüder Grimm geboren wurden.

As if from a fairy tale, castle and park Philippsruhe in Hanau, the birthplace of the brothers Grimm.

Vom Main geht der Blick Richtung Hanauer Innenstadt.
The view reaches across the Main towards downtown Hanau.

Auch Hanau – hier der Mainhafen – ist ein wichtiges Wirtschaftszentrum der Region.

Hanau – here the port of Main – is also an important economic center of the region.

Nahe Hanau liegt direkt am Main das Kraftwerk Staudinger.

The Staudinger power plant is located near Hanau, directly by the Main.

Beschaulich wirkende Frühlingsstimmung wie im Hanauer Stadtteil Klein-Auheim ...
Peaceful spring mood like here in Klein-Auheim, a district of Hanau ...

… und der Motorenlärm der Straßen (hier an der Autobahnraststätte „Taunusblick") – das Rhein-Main-Gebiet weist viele Gegensätze auf.
… and the engine noise of the streets (here at the freeway restaurant "Taunusblick") – the Rhine-Main area has many contrasts.

Schloss Johannisburg, zu Beginn des 17. Jahrhunderts errichtet, ist das Wahrzeichen von Aschaffenburg.
Johannisburg Castle, built in the early 17th century, is the landmark of Aschaffenburg.

Die am Main gelegene Stadt gehört zwar schon zum Bundesland Bayern, doch nach Hessen und in den Raum Frankfurt ist es nicht weit.
The city along the Main belongs to the state of Bavaria, but the way to Hesse and the Frankfurt area is not long.

Der Main westlich des Frankfurter Zentrums: Bei Griesheim wird sein Fluss von einer Staustufe aufgehalten.
The Main to the west of Frankfurt's center: the flow is stopped by a barrage in Griesheim.

Warum die größte Sportstätte der Region einst „Waldstadion" hieß (Bildhintergrund), wird beim Blick über Schwanheim und Niederrad deutlich. Heute nennt sich die Anlage, in der auch Eintracht Frankfurt seinen Heimspiele austrägt, „Commerzbank-Arena".

Why the largest sports complex in the region was once called "Forest Station" (background), becomes apparent with the view of Schwanheim and Niederrad. Currently named "Commerzbank-Arena", the facility is now home to Eintracht Frankfurt.

Seit vielen Jahrzehnten ist Höchst einer der wichtigsten Industriestandorte Deutschlands.

For many decades, Höchst has been one of the most important industrial locations in Germany.

Auch hier bildet der Fluss einen der vielen Vorteile, die der Industriepark zu bieten hat.

Even here, the river is one of the many advantages that the industrial park has to offer.

Von Höchst geht der Blick über Kelsterbach zum Frankfurter Flughafen.
The view wanders from Höchst across Kelsterbach toward the Frankfurt Airport.

Freizeitgestaltung in Frankfurt: Auch hier gibt es – wie in Rödelheim – große Kleingartenanlagen.
Leisure activities in Frankfurt: just like Rödelheim – many large allotment gardens.

Gleichfalls in Rödelheim befindet sich das „Brentanobad“.
Also in Rödelheim – the “Brentanobad”.

BBF

Seit 1930 kann im „Brentanobad" geschwommen werden. Die Anlage – größte ihrer Art in Frankfurt – entstand in einem Altarm des Flüsschens Nidda.

Swimming has been permitted in the "Brentanobad" since 1930. The complex – largest of its kind in Frankfurt – originated from an oxbow of the river Nidda.

Es gibt etwas, das die Hochhäuser Frankfurts weit überragt: der Taunus.

There's something that rises far above the skyscrapers of Frankfurt: the Taunus.

Wie der Name schon ahnen lässt: Der Kurbetrieb spielt in Bad Homburg vor der Höhe eine große Rolle – und das seit dem 19. Jahrhundert …

As the name implies: The spa in Bad Homburg vor der Höhe is very important (hence the prefix "Bad", bath) – ever since the 19th century …

… Eine von vielen Sehenswürdigkeiten des am Taunus gelegenen Bades ist das Landgrafenschloss samt weitläufigem Park.

… One of the many attractions by the bath near the Taunus is the Landgrafenschloss with its extensive park.

Oberursel ist bekannt für seine malerische Altstadt, über der die Kirche St. Ursula thront.

Oberursel is known for its picturesque old town, crowned by the St. Ursula Church.

Am Fuße des Taunus liegt Kronberg – Luftkurort und beliebtes Ambiente für nicht gerade arme Menschen.
In the foothills of the Taunus lies Kronberg – health resort and popular setting for the not so poor people.

In Schloss Friedrichshof, vollendet 1893, ist heute ein nobles Grandhotel samt Golfplatz im angrenzenden Park untergebracht.
The Schloss Friedrichshof which was completed in 1893, is a classy Grand Hotel with a golf course in the adjacent park today.

Für Alexander von Humboldt war der Taunus das schönste Mittelgebirge der Welt – und der weit Gereiste sollte gewusst haben, wovon er sprach.

Alexander von Humboldt found the Taunus to be the most beautiful low mountain range of the world – and the widely traveled man should have known what he was talking about.

Im Naturpark Taunus, nahe Oberursel, liegt der Kolbenberg – und auf ihm steht eine Fernmeldeanlage.
In the Taunus Nature Park, near Oberursel, lies the Kolbenberg. On top of it is a telecommunications installation.

Der Fernmeldeturm bei Taunusstein ist nach dem Berg benannt, auf dem er errichtet wurde: Hohe Wurzel.
The telecommunication tower in Taunusstein is named after the mountain on which it was built: Hohe Wurzel.

Als im 19. Jahrhundert Kur- und Heilbehandlungen in Mode kamen, wurde Königstein im Taunus schnell zu einem beliebten Ziel – und blieb es bis in die Gegenwart.

In the 19th century, spa and curative treatments became fashionable and as such Königstein quickly became a popular destination – and remained so until the present day.

Aber auch als Wohnort ist Königstein sehr gefragt. Leben in der Natur, aber nahe von Frankfurt …

Simultaneously, Königstein is also in great demand as a place of residence. Life close to nature but also close to Frankfurt …

Wahrzeichen der Stadt ist die Burg Königstein, deren älteste sichtbar erhaltenen Teile auf das 12. Jahrhundert zurückgehen.
Landmark of the city is the castle Königstein, of which the oldest visible pieces date back to the 12th century.

Taunus und – nördlicher gelegen – der Westerwald: Erholungsräume für die im Rhein-Main-Gebiet lebenden und arbeitenden Menschen sind nah und groß.

Taunus and – further north – the Westerwald: recreational areas for the people living and working in the Rhine-Main region are close and large.

Kelkheim, am Fuße des Taunus gelegen, ist eine junge Stadt. Dominiert wird sie von der Kirche des ehemaligen Franziskanerklosters (unten rechts)

Kelkheim, located at the foothills of the Taunus, is a young city. It is dominated by the church of the former Fanciscan monastary (bottom right).

Der Große Feldberg ist mit etwa 880 Metern der höchste Berg des Taunus.
The Großer Feldberg is the highest mountain of the Taunus with about 880 meters.

Die Autobahn 3 – hier bei Niederjosbach – verbindet den Rhein-Main-Raum mit Bonn, Köln und dem Ruhrgebiet.
The Autobahn 3 – here at Niederjosbach – connects the Rhine-Main area with Bonn, Cologne and the Ruhr.

Direkt neben der A 3 verläuft die neue Schnellfahrstrecke der Deutschen Bahn – so auch bei Niedernhausen.
Located directly next to the A 3, and near Niedernhausen, is where the new high-speed line of the Deutsche Bahn runs past.

Nirgendwo in Deutschland liegen zwei Landeshauptstädte derart nah beieinander. Mainz, Sitz der Regierung von Rheinland-Pfalz, ist kaum mehr als eine Flussbreite von Hessens Landeshauptstadt Wiesbaden (oben) entfernt.

Two state capital cities aren't located so close to each other anywhere else in Germany. Mainz, the seat of the government of Rheinland-Pfalz, is little more than a rivers width away from the capital of Hesse, Wiesbaden (above).

Einer der zentralen Plätze Wiesbadens ist das Dern'sche Gelände.
Seinen nördlichen Abschluss bilden das Neue Rathaus und die Marktkirche.

One of the central places of Wiesbaden is the Dern'sche Gelände.
To the north it is bordered by the new town hall and the market church.

Das Kurhaus in Wiesbaden mit dem vorgelagerten Bowling Green ist das gesellschaftliche Zentrum der Stadt. Hier ist u. a. die Spielbank beheimatet.

The Kurhaus in Wiesbaden with the Bowling Green in front is the social center of the city. Among other things, also the home of the arcade.

Viertel mit enger städtischer Bebauung – wie hier im Westend im Bereich des Blücherplatzes – sind in Wiesbaden genauso zu finden …

District with close urban development – for instance in the Westend in the area of the Blücherplatz – can be found in Wiesbaden as well …

… wie ausgedehnte Gebiete mit Villen, so nahe der Russischen Kirche.
… as extensive areas with villas, such as close to the Russian Church.

Religiöse Orte: Bei Langenhain befindet sich das Bahá'í-Haus der Andacht …
Religious places: The Bahá'í House of Worship is found in Langenhain …

… und in Wiesbaden die Russische Kirche auf dem Neroberg.

… and in Wiesbaden the Russian Church on the Neroberg.

Nördlich von Mainz liegen mehrere Inseln im Flussbett – so auch die Mariannenaue bei Eltville …
There are several islands along the river bed to the north of Mainz – such as the Mariannenaue near Eltville …

... deren Bepflanzung gerade im Frühjahr zauberhaft wirken kann.

... where the bloom is especially magical during spring.

Der Rhein bei Eltville – hier ahnt man bereits das romantische Tal, in das der Fluss gleich fließen wird und dass ihn zu einem bis heute beliebten Reiseziel gemacht hat.

The Rhine near Eltville – one can already imagine the romantic valley into which the river will flow. This makes it a popular travel destination even today.

Rheinaufwärts geht der Blick über Budenheim Richtung Mainz.
Upriver the view reaches across Budenheim to Mainz.

Nicht nur äußerlich ist er eine imposante Erscheinung – der Mainzer Dom.
Auf eine über 1000-jährige Geschichte kann die Bischofskirche zurückschauen.

Not only from the outside, the Mainz Cathedral is an imposing figure.
The bishop's church has over 1000 years of history.

Mainz stellt das politische Zentrum von Rheinland-Pfalz dar, ist jedoch nicht nur Landeshauptstadt, sondern auch Sitz einer großen Universität.

Mainz is the political center of Rheinland-Palatinate, however it is not only the state capital, it is also the seat of a major university.

Auf dem Mainzer Lerchenberg hat das ZDF sein Sendezentrum.
The ZDF has its broadcasting center on the Lerchenberg in Mainz.

Auch Mainz hat seinen Industriehafen.

Mainz also has an industrial harbor.

Als „Eventlocation“ wird die neu errichtete „Pyramide Mainz“ bei Hechtsheim vermarket.

The newly built „Pyramide Mainz“ is marketed as the event location in Hechtsheim.

Nach über 500 Kilometern mündet der Main bei Mainz in den Rhein.
After more than 500 kilometers the Main flows into the Rhine near Mainz.

Auch bei Ginsheim bildet der Rhein die Grenze zwischen Rheinland-Pfalz und Hessen.
In Ginsheim the Rhine also forms the border between Rhineland-Palatinate and Hesse.

Die Rheinfähre Landskrone überquert bei Nierstein den Fluss.
Near Nierstein the Rhine-ferry Landskrone crosses the river.

Südlich von Mainz finden sich viele alte Rheinarme, so auch bei Riedstadt-Erfelden

There are many old Rhine-branches to the south of Mainz, such as in Riedstadt-Erfelden.

Landschaftsstrukturen
bei Mainz-Finthen ...

Landscape structures
near Mainz-Finthen ...

… Wenn das Licht richtig steht, könnte man den Eindruck gewinnen, die Toskana läge in Rheinland-Pfalz.

… If the lighting is right, you might get the impression the Tuscany is in Rhineland-Palatinate.

Oppenheim, malerisch am Rhein gelegen, wird von der Katharinenkirche überragt.
Oppenheim, picturesquely placed on the Rhine, is dominated by the St. Catherine's Church.

Um 1580 entstand das Jagdschloss Kranichstein. Heute ist hier – im Nordosten Darmstadts – ein Hotel samt Museum untergebracht.

The hunting lodge Kranichstein was built around 1580. Today – here in the northeast of Darmstadt – a museum and a hotel are placed in the lodge.

Zur Anlage in Kranichstein gehört auch das sich über 112 Meter erstreckende historische Zeughaus.

The complex in Kranichstein also includes an over 112 meters long historical armory.

Seit 1997 trägt Darmstadt den Titel Wissenschaftsstadt – zu Recht, sind doch hier zahlreiche Bildungs- und Forschungseinrichtungen beheimatet.

Since 1997, the city Darmstadt has the title „Wissenschaftsstadt" (sciencecity). And justifiably so, as it houses numerous educational and research institutions.

Das Hessische Landesmuseum, untergebracht in einem 1906 vollendeten Bau, steht im Stadtzentrum von Darmstadt. Das Spektrum der Sammlungen ist groß und reicht von naturkundlichen bis zu kunst- und kulturgeschichtlichen Exponaten.

In the center of Darmstadt is the Hessian State Museum, which is situated in a building that completed construction in 1906. The range of collections is large, ranging from natural history, to art and cultural exhibits.

Mitten auf dem Darmstädter Luisenplatz steht das Ludwigsmonument. In schwindelregender Höhe von fast 40 Metern blickt Großherzog Ludewig I. auf das geschäftige Treiben in seiner ehemaligen Residenz.

The Ludwig Monument is located in the middle of the Darmstadt Luisenplatz. From a dizzying height of nearly 40 meters Grand Duke Ludewig I overlooks the hustle and bustle of his old residence.

Direkt neben dem Herrngarten liegt der Prinz-Georgs-Garten. Im zugehörigen Palais ist das Porzellanmuseum Darmstadt untergebracht.

The Prince George's Garden is placed directly next to the Herrengarten. The accompanying Palais is home to the Porcelain Museum of Darmstadt.

Hochzeitsturm, Künstlerkolonie, Ausstellungsgebäude, Platanenhain, Russische Kapelle, Künstlerhäuser, Zentrum des Jugendstils – die Mathildenhöhe Darmstadt ist ein faszinierendes Gesamtkunstwerk (Foto: Nikolaus Heiss).

Wedding tower, artist colony, exhibition building, Platanenhain, Russian Chapel, artists' houses, center of the Art Nouveau- the Mathildenhöhe in Darmstadt is a fascinating work of art (photo: Nikolaus Heiss).

Jochen Knobloch, geboren 1941 in Dresden, ist seit 1966 als freier Fotograf tätig. Von ihm sind zahlreiche Bildbände im Hinstorff Verlag erschienen.

Sabine Beil, geboren in Hanau, aufgewachsen im Taunus, studierte in Mainz und Freiburg. Viele Jahre lebte sie in Darmstadt, ehe sie nach Niedersachsen zog.

Seite 1: Die Russische Kirche auf dem Neroberg in Wiesbaden wurde 1855 vollendet.
The Russian Church on the Neroberg in Wiesbaden was completed in 1855.
Seiten 2/3: Schon der Himmel über Frankfurt zeigt, dass sich hier Deutschlands wichtigstes Flugdrehkreuz befindet.
The sky over Frankfurt shows that this is Germany's most important air hub.

Liebe Leserin, lieber Leser, wie hat Ihnen die Lektüre gefallen? Wir freuen uns über Ihre Bewertung im Internet!

Die Deutsche Nationalbibliothek verzeichnet diese Publikation in der Deutschen Nationalbibliografie; detaillierte bibliografische Daten sind im Internet über http://dnb.ddb.de abrufbar.

Lagerstraße 7 | 18055 Rostock
www.hinstorff.de

1. Auflage 2016

Herstellung: Hinstorff Verlag GmbH
Lektorat: Thomas Gallien
Karte: Stefan Jarmer
Druck und Bindung: Grafisches Centrum Cuno GmbH & Co. KG
Printed in Germany
ISBN 978-3-356-01930-8